SALT-SPRAYED BURGH

A View of Anstruther

SALT-SPRAYED BURGH

A View of Anstruther

by

FORBES MACGREGOR

Introduction

MANY excellent books have been written on Fife and many more will continue to be produced. There is still a rich mine of story and quaint fact to be exploited, for Fife's history extends back into heathen times and covers a very long chain of political, economic and religious revolutions.

This small book is merely intended to give a series of views on events and persons, chiefly as these concern Anstruther Wester, and especially the Kirk and Manse, the double-chambered heart of that closely-knit community.

I have given precedence to historical facts, minor as well as major, dealing as much with flesh and blood stories of human drama as with earth-shaking events. To sift these out from legends and hearsay was not easy, but it was rewarding to arrive as near as possible at the truth. The true story will perhaps never be revealed, because of deliberate suppression, or perversion of events, it being the first business of conquerors to serve themselves heirs to the traditions and achievements of those they had overcome, and to superimpose their own language on that of the conquered. This happened repeatedly in Fife, as in the rest of Scotland, and generally over the earth.

The Roman and Greek historians, (Tacitus, Dio Casssius and Ptolemy) gave their own versions of the Caledonians and Picts ; the Venerable Bede, who never ventured out of Northumbria, gave his biased story ; then the Gaelic Scots took over the Pictish culture of Fife and the North-East, and imposed their language and customs on the area ; the Anglo-Normans, allied with the Roman Church, superseded the Culdees and their early Celtic saints ; the Presbyterians, incited by Knox, drove out the Catholic orders (though they did not drive out all the priests, many of whom merely turned presbyter, and stayed on) ; during the civil wars and for long after them, the Presbyterians, Episcopalians and Catholics fought and intrigued for supremacy ; and, as my tale unfolds, we shall see how, as distinct from these domestic squabbles, the political interference of England brought ruin to the prosperity of the East Neuk, and reduced to a sad memory its age-long enjoyment of trade, rich agriculture and fisheries.

Much of the evidence of the truth of this story remains to this day. Visitors to Fife may see it for themselves, thanks to the preservation societies ; " What can't speak can't lie."

What many visitors, and perhaps some Fifers as well, don't realise, is the great importance of Fife all through the Christian era, or, at least, from the introduction of Christianity to Britain. Unlike many unconverted tribes of Europe, including some of Britain, the aboriginal Caledonians of Fife and its neighbouring provinces were so receptive of the new message that their former religion seems almost to have been based on the same principles. There is no record of martyrdoms inflicted by the Picts on the early missionaries, as there was, notoriously, by the Gaels, Anglo-Saxons and Norse. Many of our most prominent and influential churchmen, from the early Celtic saints like Ninian and Fillan, to later ecclesiasts such as the two Melvilles and Chalmers, have had close associations with the East Neuk. John Knox was not a Fife native ; he was born in the Gifford-gate, Haddington, in the old Anglian province of Lothian, and this probably accounts for his fiery humour.

It seems fitting that this book should be pivoted on the spiritually tough heart of Anstruther, the ancient kirk that still stands, defying time, waves, winds, storms and vandals, close by the Dreel Burn ; with it are most closely associated the manses that housed many remarkable ministers over nearly four centuries. References, too, are necessary to the equally venerable church foundations of St. Monan's, Pittenweem, Anstruther Easter, Kilrenny and others farther afield.

But church matters are the least bulky part of our story. It also concerns the lives of the ordinary, and extraordinary, folk with their ups and downs of fortune, their farces, dramas and tragedies. Even the ministers, try as they might, were not superhuman ; despite their prominence they often had to descend to the mundane businesses of wars, rebellions, love-affairs, scandals, money and even illegal transactions ; indeed every sort of exciting adventure, foreign and domestic.

Contents

Chapter I

PAGAN PICTS

ANSTRUTHER, like several East Fife towns, is very ancient. It was probably a Caledonian or Pictish settlement, several centuries B.C., long before the Roman invasions of Britain. According to Tacitus, (the son-in-law and historian of Agricola, the Roman general) after the battle of the Grampians in 84 A.D. the legions " returned to the confines of the Horestii," that is to say in the territory of the tribe that inhabited Fife at that time. The Horestii did not long remain the name of the inhabitants of Fife. In the time of Ptolemy, who wrote an account of the area, as well as of all Britain, about a century after Agricola's invasion, the name of the people was the Verturiones. These were a large mixed tribe (some of British origin, driven north by the Romans) whose territory included Fife, and a large part of Forfar, Kincardine and Perthshire. Some centuries later, when the first missionaries entered Pictland, they found it divided into seven provinces of which the most southerly was Fife, spelt in Celtic Fibh. It was a sub-kingdom of Pictavia, ruled over by a Maormor or Thegn. The Thegn or Thane of Fife was of the line of Macduff. Next to the elected king of the Picts he was the most powerful. His was always the right (when the elected high king placed his foot on the Pictish crowning-stone) to put the plain gold circlet on the king's head : the right to lead the army into battle : the right to have his relatives exempted from execution should they commit manslaughter. MacDuff's Cross was a stone pillar on the ridge of hills two miles south of Abernethy, to which MacDuff's hot tempered relatives had to flee for sanctity. Fife, on account of its early political eminence was, and is, known simply as " The Kingdom."

In Roman times the Horestii, after they had been subdued in battle by the legions, became " clients " or allies of the invaders, as also were the Otadini, another powerful British tribe on the southern shores of the Forth, whose territory stretched for a hundred miles from the East Lothian Tyne to the Northumberland Tyne. As long as these tribes accepted the Roman conditions, and supplied the legions with corn and other provisions, and perhaps helped them to manufacture some of the equipment needed for the infantry and cavalry, they were permitted to live peacefully. The Horestii, as we know from the remains of hill-terraces and from objects occasionally dug up there, cultivated the lighter soil of the coastal fringe and dry hill-slopes. They kept sheep and cattle and small hardy horses, poultry and bees. They owned dogs and cats.

Like the rest of the world at that time, before the coming of Christ, they were governed by their own customs and religion, described generally as paganism. But although they had as yet no knowledge of Christian principles, they were not necessarily given to atrocities, although their enemies often accused them of living in a barbarous state. As long as they were subject to Roman law they had to be well-behaved, for the Roman code, if just, was stern, and mercy was only very occasionally shown. The Romans also kept many hostages to ensure the good behaviour of the native tribes. The Picts were very skilled in all sorts of crafts, especially stone-carving and metal-founding, and made their own brooches, buckles, horse-harness, tools, weapons and fishing implements. Their boats were very sea-worthy though perhaps very frail in our eyes. Some of the early Pictish missionaries and monks reached as far afield as Iceland. In the prosperous days of the Picts, before the Danes and Vikings attacked them, they had a navy of several hundred sailing-ships.

Their small towns were situated on defensible positions, either on such hill-tops as Dunino, or Kelly Law, or on cliff-tops in proximity to caves. These fortified places were called " Dun " or " Pit ", followed by a description. " Pit " place-names are very numerous in East Fife, especially in the country-side behind Anstruther. Some of these are : Pittenweem, (in Celtic Pit-an-uamh, settlement of the cave,) Pitcorthy, Pitterthy, Pitkeirie. In a map of 1645 can be seen four farms near Anstruther named Pitcorthy. The explanation of this frequent occurrence of the name is that in ancient Pictish times a corthy was a circular building of stone, always roofless, which served as a community centre to which the people were called for religious ceremonies or tribal conferences.

In these corthies justice was dispensed and differences were settled without personal violence. Often people met there to listen to bards either praising or reviling those they thought deserved it. An ancient Celtic proverb says, " There is no roof in the house of mocking."

Bal and Dun were also prefixes meaning habitations, but Pit was a peculiarly Pictish description and is only to be found in the old Pictish territory of the Verturiones, as far afield as Pitlochrie, Pittodrie and Pittencrieff.

The Romans were not long able to remain north of the Forth. Once or twice at intervals, perhaps of a century, when everyone imagined they had disappeared for ever, they invaded the Pictish country in strength, terrorising, murdering and vandalising, and, in a famous phrase, " making a desert and calling it peace." Eventually, while the Picts were still heathens, the legions found them too hot to handle, and retired behind the great wall of Hadrian, not, however, before they had lost a whole legion, the Ninth, of which no trace was seen or heard, after it set off into the Caledonian Forest. It may, perhaps, have been mainly composed of non-italian tribesmen who rebelled against and got rid of their Roman officers.

The Romans left all Britain to its own devices about the year 400 and it fell into the anarchy of the Dark Ages, with jungle warfare between barbarians. Luckily for Fife and all the area now Scotland, Christianity had by this time been carried through the tribes by zealous missionaries. As I am describing these early days in the Anstruther area I should perhaps state briefly the source and movements of the new gospel. There had been Christian converts, and, unhappily, martyrs also, like St. Alban, in Roman Britain, but a knowledge of the gospel was widespread from the far south to Dumbarton, the old capital of the Strathclyde Britons. One of the first British missionaries was St. Ninian. Others were St. Mungo, and St. Patrick. In alliance with the Pictish Christians of Ulster and Leinster, in whose country was the monastery of Bangor the Great, these Irish Picts, collaborating with their British churchmen, carried out a great evangelising mission all along the East Coast of Scotland from Fife to the Shetlands. Although this was done for many years, as long ago as the 5th century, (before Columba was born) there are still extensive traces of it in ancient foundations over the whole area.

Fife in particular still perpetuates the labours of these early churchmen. As I hinted in my introduction their work was made easy for a double reason. The Picts whether under the old name of Horestii, or the later names of Verturiones, or folk of Fibh, were of a sane and receptive character ; subsequently, as such, they welcomed the new evangel, which, of course, was made more easily intelligible to them because their language was closely akin to the British of Strathclyde, (a form of Welsh) and the Pictish of Ireland. On the other hand, on the Atlantic coast, St. Patrick with his followers went to convert the Gaels in Central Ireland and found quite the reverse. The Gaels could not understand his language and showed their underlying savagery by forcing his followers waist-deep into a cold river and flogging them. The adoption of St. Patrick as patron saint of Ireland is a mysterious phenomenon which perhaps psychiatrists can explain.

Chapter II

COMING OF THE CULDEES

WE come now to particulars of these early Fife saints and the churches they founded in the Anstruther area.

The name of St. Ethernan is perpetuated in Kilrenny or Cil-Ethrenie, the cell or chapel of St. Ethernan. So says the Rev. Archibald Scott in his much researched, though rather biased, work on the Pictish Church and Nation. An equally erudite historian, the Rev. Hew Scott, a former minister of Anstruther Wester, stated, in an older account of Kilrenny, that it was founded by St. Ernan, an uncle of St. Columba. But Archibald Scott denies this and argues that the Gaelic or Columban Church had no early association with Fife, which was entirely under Pictish or British missionaries.

St. Riaghal (pronounced Rule and falsely latinised to Regulus, a rule), was the Pict associated with Kilrymont in Mucros (now St. Andrews).

St. Monance or St. Monan's (locally pronounced S'-mo-nins), according to Archibald Scott, was originally dedicated to an Irish lady of noble birth, educated at Candida Casa, or Whithorn, in Wigtownshire. Her christened name was Darerca, but her name of endearment, or pet name, such as all these early missionaries rejoiced in, was Mo'enna or Mo'ninne. Clearly the local pronunciation perpetuates this lady. There was also an early cill or small church devoted to this lady near Fife Ness. In a 1645 map it is named Kilmonen. To prove that St. Monance was a lady one need only go to the early records of Edinburgh. In the Old Town St. Monans Wynd was so named because a chapel there was dedicated to St. Monan or Mennan and the Close was named Lady Minnan's or Lady Menzies or Lady Minnes Close.

Pittenweem, or Pit-an-uamh, settlement by the cave, was founded as a religious institution, or muinntir, by St. Ninian himself from his chief centre in Whithorn. As he died on 432 A.D. this gives an exact idea of the great antiquity of the Pittenweem community. In 432 Rome was a ruin, and Attila and his Huns were on the move. Paris did not have a single church until 509, when King Clovis was converted. Canterbury was not able to boast any Christian bulding until 597. But Pittenweem had already been an evangelising centre for two centuries. As Columba did not land in Iona until 563, Pittenweem is over a century older, as a " cradle " of Christianity. Well may tourists, and natives alike, visit the Priory and cave of Pittenweem with reverence. One of the early Abs, or Abbots, was St. Fillan, not to be confused with earlier St. Fillans, one of whom lived and laboured in Strathearn, and owned the magnificent crozier of elaborate metalwork to be seen in the Scottish National Museum of Antiquities. The native Fifer, St. Fillan, spent his days and nights copying out scripture and sacred writings. A monkish legend says that his right arm gave off a luminous aura, and thereby no doubt saved the monastery many pounds of candles.

The founder of Anstruther was St. Ethernan. On this fact both Hew Scott and Archibald Scott are for once agreed. They quote old documents to prove it. The Pictish Church did not idolise saints ; they only revered them for their character and work, so all the above church foundations are only associated with their founders and abbots. There were no bishops in the early Pictish or Culdee Church, as there were in the Roman Church.

It was in the Kirk of Crail that John Knox preached the fiery sermon exhorting his congregation to "ding doon the nests and the craws will flee awa'." Then, armed with ladders, hammers and spades, the mob was led by John Knox to demolish the Roman Catholic abbeys, churches and priories in the East Neuk. But they failed to demolish the fabulous names and false legends associated with them. Robert Chambers, in " Picture of Scotland ", published in 1827, says sarcastically " that our ancestors were imposed upon some centuries back by a set of designing old gentlemen with cowls on their heads and very authoritative-looking black gowns." These would be Benedictines and Dominicans, but other orders wore grey, white and red. Their name was legion, and their legends also.

When the Culdees, or Pictish churchmen, were finally superseded by the Roman Church in the 12th-13th century, Fife, which was their last stronghold, was given over to their successors, and all the early saints and missionaries were deliberately obscured and fabulous names superimposed. Of such are Regulus, Monan and Adrian. To take them in order, (as they are all of those " whose habitation is in the air ") let us start with Regulus. As I said above, his name is based on a false derivation from St. Riaghul, the historical Celtic founder of the St. Andrews establishment. There have been notables named Regulus, which in Latin means a prince or sub-king, not a rule. The first was perhaps the Roman patriot of three centuries before Christ. There was a bishop of Senlis, near Paris, named St. Regulus, in the 8th century, but he never came near

Fife. St. Monan is pure invention, if he is described as a man. As I particularised above, St. Monan was a lady. I trust that her claims will be strenuously supported by all of her sex.

We come now to St. Adrian, and here we have a very interesting story which has taken me much time and trouble to extricate from the confusion of the past.

The Roman Emperor, Elius Hadrianus or Adrianus, was the most famous or infamous bearer of that name. He so hated the Jews that, when he found these devout and unhappy people revisiting the desolation that had once been Jerusalem, he built a new city upon the exact site of Mount Calvary and named it after himself, Elia Capitolana. To show his contempt for the Jews he erected a marble statue of a swine over the gate leading to Bethlehem. Any Jew approaching Elia, or even viewing it from a distance, was crucified. Multitudes of Jews had their ears cropped, were branded as slaves and taken in bands to the remotest parts of the Empire, which comprised almost all of the known world. Probably, in the anti-Jewish atmosphere of Christendom, the above behaviour explains the popularity of Adrian's name. An Abbot of Canterbury about 700 was named Adrian ; so were six Popes. All these probably suggested the prestigious name Adrian to supersede the historical saint Ethernan. Yet, the St. Adrian, Bishop of St. Andrews, has a certain basis, frail and almost unsupportable, ...

The Roman Catholic cell that was tolerated in St. Andrews, and which had been introduced in 761 into the Pictish foundation of Kilrymont, may have had a " bishop " styled Adrian, but this title, Bishop, which had been introduced into Scotland by Kenneth MacAlpine, was not recognised by either the Columban or the Pictish Church. This obscure and unpopular Adrian, if he ever can be proved to have existed, was later blown up to great proportions when the Roman Church took over in the 12th century.

As for the tale of the martyrdom of St. Monan and St. Adrian, with 6000 others, perhaps on the May Island, this is the sort of inflated fable that was fed to the gullible for centuries. On the May Island there was a Culdee religious cell, named a disert. (Dysart near Kirkcaldy was originally one of these). It meant a remote place where a holy man lived in meditation. Handfuls of recluses may easily have been martyred by pirates on the May, on several occasions from the time of Ninian, around 400, when he founded this disert. But as the raids of the " Gentiles ", or heathen Norse, did not begin until the end of the 8th century, it is not at all likely that St. Monan or Moninne, who lived in the 6th century, was martyred. Adrian, if he existed, may have been martyred, for his date is given as the middle of the 9th century. But 6000 martyrs ! The greatest historical martyrdom in Britain was at Chester in 613, when the heathen Anglian King Ethelfrid massacred about 1200 monks.

The murder of 68 Columban monks on Iona by Vikings in 806 was considered a great " red martyrdom." Perhaps the 6000 martyrs of the May was an attempt to compete with the 11,000 martyred virgins of Cologne led by St. Ursula, which on investigation cannot even be traced to one poor little virgin.

All this, of course, does not affect the traditions of St. Adrian's Church, which extend back for several centuries. But, as far as the old kirk of Anstruther Wester is concerned, it is of little consequence whether it be named St. Ethernan's, St. Adrian's, St. Mungo's or St. Bingo's. Its days as a kirk seem to be over. It still stands solidly on its rocky headland above the Dreel, perhaps enjoying stony dreams of ancient glories, of the fiery eloquence of Knox who preached in it, or of other battles, wordy or bloody, long ago.

Chapter III

STORM—SWEPT BURGH

This ancient Kirk is the tough heart of Auld Anster. Although the town is probably much older than this 7th century foundation of St. Ethernan, it is around this building and its predecessors that much of the life of the town has centred, and from its inspiration sons of Anstruther have gone out to battle in the wide and often hostile or indifferent world.

In the oldest written records, in the reign of William 1, the Lion, (1165-1214) Anstruther was written Kynstruther. This is an anglified spelling of the Gaelic place-name, Gaelic having displaced Pictish soon after the forced union of the Picts in the 9th century. In Gaelic the name is ceann an struth, the headland by the small stream. In the map of 1645 mentioned above, the well-known Kincraig, the caravan-site near Elie, is spelt Kean Craige, almost pure Gaelic. Another caravan-site near St. Andrews is similarly spelt Keankell, now Kinkell. The phrase, " headland by the small stream," described the position of Anstruther, but is most aptly applied to the site of the Old Kirk.

The rocky promontory above the Dreel, or Anster Burn, as it is also called, is occupied by the Old Kirk of Anstruther and its churchyard, kirkyard or kirkgreen, which is half-surrounded by the sea at high tides. The kirkyard lies between the kirk and the shore and is necessarily supported from the undermining fury of the ocean by a strong bulwark or kirk-dyke. No kirkyard could be nearer the sea. It seems almost as if those in their last sleep wished to hear the roar of the ocean into eternity.

On the same headland, inland to the south and west of the kirk, are the oldest houses still standing in the burgh, as well as many of the most recently built. Several old houses have lintels dated from the mid-seventeenth century when Cromwell's army devastated the town and desecrated the kirk, an invariable custom of these puritanical levellers. They stabled their horses in God's house and lit their church-warden pipes with strips torn from the bible. As the session records of Anstruther Wester and Easter tell, they tossed the pulpit bible into the sea, incurring the burgh in the trouble of drying it out and, later, the expense of replacing it. They also destroyed the sermon-glass or hour-glass. A self-sacrificing lady of the parish sold some of her possessions to redeem the sacramental silver from these holy vandals.

The group of houses, comprising the White House, and a smaller intermediate house dated 1718, and the Old Manse of 1703, stand even nearer to the open sea than the kirk : so near, indeed, that their gardens and offices have to be protected from the storms by massive vertical walls and aprons, founded on the skellies or strata of varied kinds of limestone. Even thus protected, only certain plants, tolerant of, or rejoicing in sea-water, such as East Lothian stock, (the gilly-flower whose clove-flavoured blossoms fill the early summer), sea-holly, sea-pinks (thrift), sea-marsh grass and that evilly-named scurvy-grass with masses of scented blooms like drifted snow, can survive the frequent drenchings of flung spray.

Unluckily, as I write this, I have to record that the terrible tempest of Hogmanay 1978 which caused much damage to Cellardyke and other East Fife towns, undermined and completely demolished the stone stable of the Old Manse, which had withstood the waves for so long.

There is also, distinct from these buildings, a quaint and attractive house, sunk into the surrounding ground close to the kirkyard : and, still adjacent to the kirkyard, another two-storeyed house of quaint style. The first-mentioned house, from the rudely-cut bas-relief by the door, either of a burning bush or of a wheat-sheaf, is probably either an ancient session-house for the kirk, or an old harbour inn.

But the first group of houses of 1703, or slightly later, although now over a quarter millennium old, is not as old as some houses also still inhabited, farther inland in the burgh ; which points to a removal, a damage, or even a destruction by the sea of predecessors which anciently stood on the Harbour Head before the present houses were built.

History records great inundations of the sea in 1625, in 1655, and in 1670, which destroyed many houses and undermined others. These disasters were followed by an even more violent storm about 1690 which carried away the Fore Street, with many warehouses and public buildings, including the Town House. The line they occupied is now an area of great jagged skellies and boulders, covered at every tide. As much of the sedimentary rock was freestone of a very durable kind, it was eminently suitable for the building of the harbour extension, last century, especially when the stratified rocks were built-in vertically, the better to resist the surface pressure of storm water. But the removal of thousands of tons of this natural barrier against the violent storms from the exposed south-east, and the reduction of the shore-level by quarrying, has made the house-bulwarks more vulnerable when the billows roll in unimpeded, having no land obstacle to break or divert their force, for four hundred miles from the Dutch and Frisian coasts. A constant vigilance is essential to detect damage to the bulwarks.

It is unlikely that the old Vicarage of pre-reformation times, or the subsequent manse, was in Fore Street. The site of the present Old Manse, on the Shore of the Old Harbour Head, or Hammer Head, being in close proximity to the Kirk, was probably the site of all residences occupied by the Roman Vicars, or their successors, the Presbyterian ministers, of Anstruther. As often happened with farmhouses and manses, as well as castles, the stones from the abandoned buildings were largely used for the new. The former foundations would be adapted, the better stones rebuilt to face the new walls, and the broken stone or rubble used to fill up the middle of these yard-thick walls.

The biggest building charges, as we know from old accounts, were for cartage or sledging of stones. It is a sad and sickening light that is cast on the bestial status of women in the Scotland of Knox and the so-called Reformers, that in Edinburgh and other " romantic towns " women were employed to drag these carts and slypes, or sledges, from the stone-quarries. We are in hope that it was not so in Anstruther, though it was general all along the coastal fishing-villages and towns for the women and girls to gather bait, and carry fish creels, with sculls on top (these combined often weighing up to two hundredweights). These female navvies were called yauds which is an elegant Scots expression for an old cow, an old horse or a jade. There is a triangle of rough heath at a cross-roads near Coldingham Moor, (visible from the East Neuk, for it stands high) which is called the " Haud Yauds ", that is, a rendezvous for the fishwives carrying their loads inland. This small circumstance is a part of the true history of Scots " democracy " in the " Good Old Days ".

To return to the manse-building. Burning and carting of lime was also a heavy charge but, to balance this, mason's labour and skill was cheap. For example, at the building of the celebrated Peebles Brig in the 16th century, a mason's day-wage was a plack, equal to an old-fashioned farthing. With it, however, a stone of oatmeal or bearmeal, could be bought, which now costs £2. A penny an hour was mason's wages throughout the 18th century ; " country-work ", i.e. rough masonry, even cheaper. But a penny was a weighty bit of copper then, with an elegant Britannia modelled on one of Charles Second's pieces de resistance, and it could be exchanged for a dozen eggs, a gill of whisky, a bag of coal or a bucket of herring.

It is a well-known scandal that many splendid buildings, the pride of mediaeval architects, (some of whom had been brought for the purpose from Italy) were destroyed by the reformers, and of course this opened the door to all and sundry to use the glory of the High Middle Ages as a free quarry to build wretched structures. It was said in some Scottish towns, as in St. Andrews, that there was " hardly a hoose in the toon but had a kirk-stane intil't," This could also be said of Anstruther, but the tower of St. Nicholas, to which I now refer, defied vandals : the priory of Pittenweem were pillaged for building materials after Knox's mob had destroyed the extensive ecclesiastic works there as well as the church of St. Monans.

The ancient church by the Dreel was, until the mid-seventeenth century, the only kirk of Anstruther. In 1634, as I particularise later, the kirk of Anstruther Easter was completed to accommodate a new parish of that name. The Kirk of Anstruther Wester, as it stands at present, is obviously of two different eras. The nave, to the east, has been three times rebuilt, each building getting smaller ; the last was in 1846. It is not, therefore, the proportionate building it originally was, when John Knox preached here in the 1560s, under a different roof.

The square, rather squat, tower of St. Nicholas belies its height. It has immensely thick walls, said to date from 1243, though some researchers do not think that many Fife churches are nearly as old as the 17th century. In the 13th century, however, the cult of St. Nicholas, the patron saint of sailors, was very popular all through Christendom, and hundreds of churches were dedicated to him. Probably St. Nicholas tower suffered severely from English invasions of Fife, for the whole edifice was repaired in the days of Sir Andrew Wood in the early 16th century, and a parapet and steeple were added. But it had to be constantly repaired and, latterly, was harled to preserve the free-stone exterior. As late as 1930 the steeple was struck by lightning in a bad storm in September of that year. The weathercock " airts ". or compass directions, are still 90° out, though this is an insignificant detail when one considers the extensive face-lift the tower has had in recent years, mainly the renovations of the clock-faces and the complete overhaul of the beautiful clockwork. Old though the tower undoubtedly is, in its originals it is very much older than the St. Nicholas era. It may have been used as a refuge during the raids of Danish and Norse sea-rovers. Their incursions went on intermittently through the 9th, 10th and 11th centuries. Although there is an old legend that Fife was avoided by the Gentiles (as the churchmen called all heathens) and became known to them as the " Graveyard of the Danes ", this is not supported by history.

In 877, for example, at Inverdovat, now a farm near Newport, the Scots King Constantine II, son of Kenneth MacAlpine, was captured, and his entire army annihilated by sea-raiders in force. It is said, traditionally, that Constantine was beheaded by the Danes in a cave near Fife Ness. If so, he would be taken there by sea to the Danish fort of which traces still exist. But the small extent of the walled fort shows that the invaders had only a precarious hold on Fife soil. Such raids as they made would only be brief. The most serious invasion of the Danes (which threatened to subdue Scotland as completely as England was to be by Sweyn in 1013) took place in 990 when Kenneth III defeated them completely at Luncarty near Perth. Any parties of Danes who wished to settle in Scotland, as many did, had to submit to the Scottish crown.

In another less massive form, the Kirk of Anstruther existed even earlier than the Viking period. St. Ethernan's foundation in the 7th century may have been a rough stone building, made of layers of freestone from the nearby skellies, but this is conjectural. Most of the Culdee churches were built of such durable woods as oak or pine. Many small foundations were known in Gaelic as dairteach or oak-houses. They may even have been composed, in wooded areas, of living oak-trees, with walls of wattle and clay, roofed with rushes or heather. Many rural churches in Scotland, before slates became available in the 17th century, were thatched. The parish kirk of Gretna was burnt down in that century by mischievous youths setting fire to the thatch as they shot muskets at the house-martins' nests under the eaves. In ancient Fife the countryside, apart from the arable coastal plain, was covered with primeval forests of oak, pine, birch and smaller trees such as hawthorn, willow, hazel and crab-apple.

When, much later, a stone church was built above the Dreel, it would be round, not square or cruciform, for the Picts, whether of Alban (Scotland) or Ireland, built circular structures. There still exist many of their brochs and hut-circles, as well as the tall, pencil-shaped Pictish towers. There is one at Abernethy, 75 feet high ; another at Brechin, 103 feet high and only 16 feet in diameter ; another at Cashel in Tipperary. They have resisted the elements and enemies for a thousand years. But the Anstruther building was probably much smaller and less durable, or more exposed to storms and attacks.

The old Celtic style of Anstruther Kirk was probably abandoned when it was rebuilt and re-dedicated about 1090 by Margaret, the English wife of Malcolm Canmore. As she had set herself the task of Anglicising Celtic Scotland, (and leaving her six sons to complete it) she began on the churches. Anstruther Kirk was squarely built in the Anglo-Saxon style with Saxon pillars and a Gothic tower. The tower was for long fitted with a cresset or basket of open iron-work, in which a beacon blazed as a signal to shipping, either to warn them off the rocky coast, or to guide them to the harbour at the mouth of the Dreel. When a lighthouse was erected on the May Island, to replace a more primitive beacon, the architect designed it on the model of St. Nicholas Tower. Although originally the

May had been a detached part of Pittenweem, (St. Ninian having at times gone from Pittenweem to reside temporarily on the disert) in the troubled times following the Reformation, both Anstruther and Crail laid claims to it. The St. Nicholas style of lighthouse was erected in the reign of Charles I. When the architect was returning the five miles to the mainland he was shipwrecked and drowned. This was put down to the malficium or evil-doing of witches, and, in the superstitious atmosphere of the 1630 period, several poor old women were " incremated " or " burnt quick," that is, alive, at Pittenweem, St. Monan's and Anstruther, for raising the storm by their spells. Their motive was put down to spite against the man who wanted to save the lives of seamen.

Before leaving the age of the Culdees it is as well to point out two permanent memorials to their influence, which no amount of ecclesiastical jealousy could efface. One is the perpetuation of the name (in Celtic, Cele De means Friends of God) in such places as Kirkcaldy, Kirk of the Culdees, and in the Caddy's (i.e. Culdees) Burn between Cellardyke and Anstruther.

Men may come and men may go but wells go on forever : many perennial springs in Fife, as elsewhere, were used by the Culdee missionaries. Their diserts, frequently in caves, had to be near a spring. These springs rarely lost their original names. St. Fillan's well is in the inner cave of Pittenweem, St. Irnie's is at Kilrenny and St. Monan's well in a cave near the village. The cave has since been destroyed but the well still flows. The site of St. Monan's was anciently named Inverey, which means the mouth of the small stream. The name is an unusual combination of Gaelic and Old Teutonic, inbhear (Gaelic) meaning mouth of the river, and eye (or ij in Dutch) meaning a gush or stream of water. This points to a very ancient settlement of Frisians here, long before the Gaelic invasion of 844, and perhaps even before the Culdees gave it the name St. Monan's three centuries earlier.

Chapter IV

TARNISHED FRINGE OF GOLD

IT is worth mention, to account for the thickly populated coastal towns of the middle ages, which for centuries formed an almost continuous line from Inverkeithing to St. Andrews, that, in the opinion of Tucker, a 17th century observer, the very fertile farmlands were inhabited only by the lairds, their farmer tenants and the peasantry. Everyone else was driven off the fertile fields " even to the very shore." There they had to find employment in fishing, in trade, or in industry. Pennant, an English traveller of the mid 18th century, said there was no stretch of British coastline that presented such a populous and continuous appearance as the south coast of Fife. But it was agricultural wealth that this primarily depended upon.

One of the most populous towns was Anstruther Easter. Originally it was part of the parish of Kilrenny but as it grew in size and prosperity it began to burst its bounds. It is supposed that, early in the 17th century, it was more populous than Glasgow which, in 1610, had about 7000 inhabitants. The parish church being over a mile away, it was suggested to build a covered alleyway to it to protect the kirkgoers when it " was not kirk-weather ", that is, when it was tempestuous. But the completion of the new kirk of Anstruther Easter in 1634 made the gallery unnecessary. James Melville, famous nephew of the equally famous Andrew Melville, (who for his obduracy spent some time in the Tower of London) became first minister of the new church.

All through the Middle Ages and into early modern times Fife was poetically and accurately described as a " beggar's mantle fringed with gold." The higher landward parts of Fife, except the Howe, or hollow, of the vale of Eden, were moorlands and forests, in some of which, (notably Mucros or the headland of the wild boars, near St. Andrews and commemorated in Boarhills) there lived at large, wild beasts ; boars, wolves, badgers, roe and red deer, foxes and otters and such small creatures as pole-cats, stoats, weasels, hedgehogs, hares, (but no rabbits until these were introduced by the Normans). Birds innumerable and amphibians and reptiles were well represented. It was a hunter's paradise, but death to agriculture. The broad coastal strips, cultivated from prehistoric times, were rich in oats, barley (or bere), beans and pease. Wheat was also grown in favourable areas. Milk cattle were kept, and oxen and cows used for yoking to the plough, the large Flemish draught horses not yet having been introduced.

A very humorous and detailed account of a 16th century Fife farm is to be read in the Scots of that time, about 1560, in the reign of Mary, Queen of Scots. The lines concerning ox-ploughing are these, (as the wife and husband agree to swop places).

Scho lowsit the oxen aucht or nine
And hynt ane gad-staff in her hand.

(She loosened the oxen eight or nine
And gripped a gad-staff in her hand.)

The poem is the " Wife of Auchtermuchty " and is of course set in the Howe of Fife, but it could well have applied to any farm in the East Neuk.

In the same century, especially, fishing for herring and white fish and shell-fish was very prosperous. In 1577, for example, an exact record by the parish minister of Dunbar, on the opposite coast over the Forth, tells us that a thousand herring-boats congregated there, drawn from many towns and villages nearby and also from Holland, to take part in the annual " drave ", or drive, upon the vast shoals of herring that frequented the area. " Herring-roads " radiating from Dunbar inland to the thickly populated Lammermuir and Merse districts are still traceable, where cadgers led their horses, laden with panniers of herring, skate, cod, ling and haddock in long convoys, to feed the townfolk, farmers, peasantry and shepherds. The Lammermuir, like the Highlands, is now cleared of small farms. Herring roads, too, crossed Fife but not to any extent. Most of the Pittenweem and Anstruther herring were, of old, salted and shipped to the Continent. The " Drave of Dunbar " is all too well remembered, for, as it turned out, a sudden storm scattered the great armada of fishers, and fourteen score were made widows overnight. The recording minister attributed this disaster to their setting off on a Sunday. But, in October 1881, as bad a disaster hit the Eyemouth fleet and widowed half the town ; on this occasion they sailed out on a Thursday. The sea does not observe religious calendars.

All the East Neuk towns shared in the wealth of coastal land and rich waters. The ministers' stipends were partly paid in grain and sometimes in " kain " i.e. cattle, sheep, poultry, sea-fowl (solan-geese) and fish. The Dreel was said to have been at one time a spawning stream for salmon and sea-trout. This seems unlikely when one looks at it today, where only eels can survive comfortably in the shallow and muddy waters. But conditions were different in earlier times. There was much marshland, bog and thick natural forest in the gathering ground of the many small tributaries of the

Dreel, which drains an area of about twenty square miles. Rainfall did not evaporate as rapidly as it does in today's open fields. Consequently the Dreel drew a steadier, purer and more copious flow, and the sequestered feeding streams at different points would be ideal for the hatching of salmon roe, and for the growth of the parr until they were ready to return to the sea. The arms of Anstruther show three salmon, as a source of revenue. But even with a reduced flow of water, in the time when the marshes and woods were destroyed, the Dreel still proved useful. As it nears the sea, it drops about fifty feet in a mile. In medieval times it drove six mills. Latterly, about 1700, one mill was fed from a mill-lade, still traceable. The water drawn from the Dreel supplied a large bucket mill-wheel for the grinding of corn. This old mill close by the Dreel Bridge was recently converted to modern houses. It had been disused for about a century.

Anstruther Wester was full of warehouses, containing grain, salt, malt, salted herrings, ling and cod. A profitable trade was carried out with the Hanseatic league and the Flemish, Dutch and Brabantine states. These " states " were fortified and independent towns, and their sea-captains probably looked on the Anstruthers, both being Royal Burghs, as equal in prestige to their own " states." On the coast of the Dutch island of Walcheren, in the small town of Veere, there is a sea-shore tavern which is still called the " Schotse Huis " or Scots House. Some years ago I visited Veere and saw the remains of the harbour and quays where the East Neuk ships tied up centuries ago and unloaded their goods for distribution to various places, after storage in the Scots House, which was a warehouse or staple. This shows the great prosperity and far-flung influence of Anstruther and kindred Fife towns, that truly formed the " fringe of gold," before they were ruined by natural and political disasters.

Although the Firth of Forth was chiefly fished by local boats in the 16th century, enormous fleets of Dutch " busses ", or broad-bottomed vessels of thirty tons burden, with two or three masts, fished, chiefly for herring, off the Shetland and North-Eastern Scottish coasts. Until the English and Spanish wars disturbed Dutch commerce, as many as 2000 busses and other vessels fished during the season for this vast rich harvest.

There was a very close racial and political tie between Fife and the Low Countries. There still remain, west of Anstruther, the great blocks of stone which were once the old Dutch harbour, showing that these foreign merchants were warmly welcomed in Anstruther. But this relationship goes much farther back in time. Many of the Scottish fishing-towns were peopled by folk whose ancestors were not Pictish, but had come from Friesland in the early middle ages, perhaps forced to leave because of incursions of the Angles and Saxons through the ancient Friesland territory. Again, in the 12th century, a disastrous series of storms broke the ancient Dutch dykes (just as in 1953 when 1200 people were drowned in Holland). Much of the land was submerged throughout the middle ages. The Zuider Zee (or South Sea) was for centuries, until recently reclaimed, a reminder of this cataclysm which drove people as far as Scotland to find a firmer foothold. The Firth of Forth was anciently known as the Mare Frisicum or Friesian Sea, because it was lined by fishing communities from that country. Shipwrecks also added to this immigrant population, for there was little chance of ship-wrecked mariners returning home. In the 16th century, for example, a Brabantine or Flemish vessel was wrecked on the Fife coast and the sailors forced to take up their habitation in what is now Buckhaven. As they spoke Flemish and could scarcely understand Fifish, they for long were the laughing-stocks of many of the unfeeling wits in Scotland. There are many foreign-sounding surnames in the East Neuk which doubtless came from survivors of these far-off disasters. But there was always a racial sympathy with Europe.

A free exchange of goods (especially silks, spices, wines and spirits in return for Fife salt, coal, woollen cloth, grain and fish), led to a good deal of high-living and conviviality even in the humblest of homes. When the unpopular Union of 1707 enforced the salt and malt taxes, and the price of all commodities dependent on these made them unavailable, there was wholesale smuggling and murderous affrays with the excise officers. Smugglers were looked on as patriots and benefactors, even by the ministers, and the Old Manse was admirably situated for reception and distribution of unexcised goods. To this day there is a low secret door on the seaward side of the Manse leading to the shore. I shall later refer to a violent incident which shows the attitude of the East Neuk folk, as of all Scots, to the new acts.

The Golden Age of warehousing and busy harbours was not to last for ever. The Civil War of 1641-5 had fatal results for Anstruther. The two royal burghs contributed levies four times as numerous as Dunfermline, for the Covenanting army : East and West Anstruther, (for they had been separate parishes a few years before) enlisted at least 60 men, Dunfermline only 15. But of the 63 men, including many seamen, who set off in 1645 against Montrose, not one was ever seen again, alive or dead. All were trapped in Kilsyth Moss by Montrose's Highlanders and shot or cut down without mercy or remorse. Three entire Fife regiments were wiped out. Henceforth for generations no Anstruther men could be induced to join any military force. But Anstruther was destined for disasters other than military ones. A series of seven cold, wet summers ended in 1699 with a great famine in Scotland, in which one third of some parishes starved to death.

This was as bad as the plague of 1645 had been, when entire hamlets were destroyed and never peopled again, both in Fife and across the Forth in Berwickshire and the Lothians. Hundreds of farms were affected and left to fall into ruin. With so many undrained moors, the rural population had always been stricken with tertian and quartian fevers. This crippling illness was due to malaria, carried from the swarms of mosquitoes that bred undisturbed. When better husbandry drained these swamps, the fevers disappeared. At sea, the fishing failed, boats were allowed to rot, and a general disinclination to spend capital on new ones aggravated the distress. The herring could appear and disappear in a mysterious way, just as they are doing now. As I said earlier, the storms of 1655 and 1670 were followed by another more violent in 1690 during the famine years of the " Seven Winters."

But worse, if worse could be imagined, came from a political quarter. The failure of the Darien Scheme ruined Fife, particularly, for most of the investment, both in money and material, came from the initiative of the merchants and lairds of that practical region. The fault was laid at the door of the London merchants who had the ear of the new Dutch king, William of Orange. But, strangely enough, when one considers the old friendship between Fife and the Low Countries, much of the blame for the Darien disaster can be laid on the opposition of the West Indian Dutch merchants to the Scottish attempt at colonisation on the Central American isthmus of Darien.

Soon afterwards came the Union of 1707, mentioned above. Salt was ultimately taxed to forty times its market value. The continental trade, as well as any share in colonial trade, was at an end for East Scotland. The beggar's mantle was fringed with tatters, however much Glasgow and the west prospered with the American trade.

Leaving Anstruther for the moment in the midst of this economic misery, we shall refresh ourselves by dipping back briefly into the vigorous lives of the ministers who had charge of the parish from the Reformation to 1700. Any blame for the decline of Anstruther could not be theirs, as their life-stories well show.

Chapter V

HOT-BED OF REBELLION

THROUGH all the stormy period from the 1560 Reformation to 1700, the ministers of Anstruther who inhabited the earlier manse, prior to the building of the present Old Manse of 1703, had been conspicuous as strong characters, frequently getting into trouble with the King and Privy Council, for insisting that Scotland was ruled by God and not an earthly power. It had been no easy task, after the Act of 1560, declaring Roman Catholicism illegal, to supply the parish with ministers. As I have said, this difficulty was got over, especially in the Highlands, by allowing the former priest to turn presbyter. In Anstruther, the Rev. William Clerk, ordained in 1565, had the extra parish charges of Kilrenny and Abercrombie, the latter being the old parish which contained St. Monan's. Clerk had married a relation of the laird, a Margaret Anstruther. His two successors, Robert Wood and James Daes tried for a time to carry the triple burden, liked it not, and were transferred to Kilrenny, a favourite Elysium for Anstruther ministers. But James Melville tried to lighten the burden. In his short term of four years he secured an incumbent for Abercrombie, leaving himself only Anstruther and Kilrenny. Then he also was transferred to Kilrenny and took up his abode there, or rather, in the western part of that parish, in the magnificent manse which his own enterprise had caused to be built. It is still inhabited, after four centuries. The Rev. George Ogg, D.D. was its eminent tenant until his death a few years ago. It is now restored to its old pristine glory and many of its former architectural features revealed. Some of these had suffered long neglect, having passed through the hands of many owners, including those of the Anstruther lairds, who added a wing. It is now tenanted by the Rev. George Miller, minister of the united triple parish.

The minister of Anstruther who followed Melville was a fire-brand named Robert Durie. After graduating M.A. at St. Andrews he went to the fortress of La Rochelle, then under siege by the Catholic party of France, incited by Catherine de Medici (mother-in-law of Mary Queen of Scots, then imprisoned in England by Elizabeth). The atrocious massacre of St. Bartholomew, upon the Huguenots in Paris in 1572, had just shocked Europe, hardened as it was. La Rochelle was the centre of Calvinist France and there Durie imbibed much of the militancy of the early reformers, who were not less prone to burning heretics than were their opponents. Knox had died in 1572, but his reforming successors were much more aggressive than even he had been.

Durie came back to Fife as a fanatical Calvinist and was inducted to Abercrombie in 1588, the Armada year. Anstruther had a rather strange encounter with the survivors of that disaster. As is well-known the Armada was pursued by the English fleet as far up the North Sea as the Firth of Forth. The Duke of Medina-Sidonia, the vice-commodore, who was not a seaman, then tried to return to Spain by the Pentland Firth and the Hebridean and Irish coasts. Adverse winds threw his galleons on to the savage rocks and more savage natives of the Atlantic coast. Medina-Sidonia was relatively lucky, his flag-ship being wrecked with little loss of life on the Fair Isle. A relative of mine, whose ancestors came from the Fair Isle, told me as a fact that the Shetland women picked fifty of the most handsome Spaniards for their mates, and lured many of the unlucky ones into a tidal bay, where they were drowned. At any rate Medina-Sidonia and many of his crew escaped these sirens and got away by pinnaces, eventually reaching Anstruther, where they sought food and shelter.

Although not at war with Spain, the Scots had been prepared to defend themselves should the Spanish army have invaded. The laird and magistrates of Anstruther, after some negotiation, generously provided for the Spaniards, on the grounds that they were compelled by Christian charity to help even enemies and religious opponents. A noble example which the bigots of the time should have copied, but conspicuously, did not.

However, some years later, when a crew of Anstruther men were cast away on the Netherlands coast, then in Spanish hands, the Anstruther kindness to Medina-Sidonia was rewarded by an equally Christian act of mercy. Medina-Sidonia in gratitude for his reception in Anstruther, left his engraved money-chest with the minister. Its carved lid was let into the lintel of the " watch-tower ", where it is still conspicuous.

Durie would perhaps not have acquiesced in this forgiveness of Catholics, but as he was not yet in Anstruther parish, he was not consulted.

He went as chaplain with the Gentlemen Adventurers of Fife, to Lewis in 1598, to colonise it ; an effort successively made on two other occasions by the Adventurers, but ending in failure and atrocity. In 1601 Durie also visited Orkney and Shetland, to carry the Calvinistic torch.

When the General Assembly, soon after, against the commands of James VI (now also James I of England), met at Aberdeen, Durie was a leading spirit. The Scots proverb made about this time, to show how little this assembly valued the royal wrath, was, " Ye may belch a whilie at the pier o' Leith afore ye raise a storm in Aiberdeen." With several others, Durie was arrested but, refusing to recant, he was thrown with his rebellious friends into Blackness Castle. At his trial in 1606, he defied the king and was exiled for life. He went to Holland with his family, where he was endowed with a reformed church in Leyden. He died in 1616, the same year as Shakespeare died.

His son, John, a youth of 18, then began to study for the ministry, probably at Leyden University, which many young Scots attended. He was made minister of the English Merchants', or Court Kirk, at Rotterdam, latterly known as the Schotse Kerk or Scots Kirk. The German dive-bombers demolished it three centuries later, in 1940, in the destruction of the centre of Rotterdam, but the records including Durie's documents were recovered, and the kirk rebuilt. I have attended services there, and wondered how many Scots remember the influence here of one of Anstruther's sons. John Durie died in 1680 aged 82, still in exile in Holland.

John Fairfoul, another graduate of St. Andrews, was inducted to Anstruther in 1610, at the mature age of 64. He had already gained a bad reputation with King James by praying in public for Durie and the other exiles, so he was soon banished. This sentence was not so severe as Durie's, for Fairfoul was only condemned to be ' confined to Dundee ' where he was apparently not able to do the damage he would have done in Anstruther. His sentence was the equivalent of the old order of banishment made on offenders by the early Stuart kings when they resided with the court in Falkland Palace ; " Go to Freuchie and fry mice." Fairfoul survived the incarceration in Dundee until he was eighty, and a year before his death in 1626, he had had the pleasure of seeing James VI and I off to his long home.

George Dewar, also a St. Andrews graduate, carried on the rebellion immediately and was " deposed for disaffection " from Anstruther. In the Civil War he was in trouble again.

St. Andrews was evidently a hotbed of rebellion, for another graduate, David Guthrie, M.A. proved to be the very opposite of the famous Vicar of Bray, who turned his coat to suit the political weather. There have been many claimants to this doubtful honour, the Vicarship of Bray, but Guthrie filled the role of an Anti-Vicar of Bray. He fell out with Cromwell by praying in the pulpit for Charles II, and was imprisoned in Edinburgh Castle. For a long time all he saw of his home, on clear days only, was Kelly Law and perhaps the smoke from the Anstruther lums, a view to make an East-Neuk man very home-sick. At the Restoration he annoyed Charles II by refusing to conform to Episcopacy, and was again punished.

Two quieter men followed during the " Killing Times," 1679 - 88, but no sooner was their successor Thomas Auchinleck, M.A. (St. Andrews) inducted in 1689, the year of Killiecrankie, than he was deposed for refusing to read the Royal Proclamation of the succession of William and Mary, or to pray for their well-being. Like many St. Andrews graduates of that era, he was a strong Episcopalian and Jacobite. He was heard of no more and was probably thought to be comfortably dead and buried. But in 1715, at the age of 60, he rose and followed Lord Panmure in the cause of the Old Pretender. On the failure of that rising he tried to occupy the pupit of Monifieth, but was evicted. He lived to be 90 and, in expiring early in 1745, he missed what would have glorified his departure, for in the late summer of that memorable year Bonnie Prince Charlie landed in Moidart to start his heroic attempt om the throne of his fathers.

Chapter VI

CALVINISTIC GLOOM

PERHAPS influenced by what he regarded as the heavy hand of God afflicting the wickedness of people, the next minister of Anstruther, (now designated, since 1634, Anstruther Wester) the Rev. Thomas Black, began, in 1700, to show signs of mental derangement. His former colleague across the Dreel, Andrew Thomson, of Anstruther Easter, from the country of the Hill Folk or Westland Whigs (Covenanters), had been overwhelmed from two sides. The " Killing Times " were at their height, following the defeat of the Cameronians at Bothwell Brig. Thomson's friends were being barbarously treated in Edinburgh, tortured, executed, or banished. Nearer home, his own parish was depressed, and, final blow, his wife, mother of six young children, was struck down suddenly.

One winter night, returning from a late visit in Anstruther Wester, probably to the Wester manse, his servant lass preceding him with a lantern across the Dreel foot-bridge, a black beast crossed their path from the direction of the graveyard. The terrified maid dropped the lantern and extinguished it. Perhaps now fully convinced that the Evil One was dogging his footsteps, on account of his ignoring the advice of his father against taking up an appointment in an established church, Thomson could take no more reverses. At any rate he was found drowned in the Dreel next morning, which was generally looked on as self-destruction, the Dreel being shallow at the time.

Thomas Black of Anstruther Wester was apparently also prone to what Professor Saintsbury called the " good old Saxon gloom." This phrase was applied to the poems of the minister, at that period, of Athelstaneford. He was Robert Blair, also related to the Covenanting folk. His masterpiece had the cheerless title " The Grave : " he revels in tombs hung with ropy slime ; only at the very end, on resurrection, is he rather optimistic. Robert Burns constantly read this poem and quoted it at length in a letter to one of his lady-loves. I am glad to say he chose the passage on " friendship "rather than some of the chilling passages which I read as a boy in my grandfather's English text-book, on which tender infants in early Victorian times had to cut their literary teeth. In these occur such descriptions as this :

> " Cheerless unsocial plant (the yew) that loves to dwell
> Midst sculls and coffins, epitaphs and worms
> Where light-heeled ghosts and visionary shades
> Beneath the wan cold moon (as fame reports)
> Embody'd thick, perform their mystic rounds."

There are many even more blood-cooling passages. For generations after Blair's early death the rustics used to swear his ghost, or that of his successor John Home, walked in a dark ravine under the Garleton Hills, which are clearly seen from the Old Manse of Anstruther Wester.

Black failed to turn up to Sunday services : month after month the congregation had to disperse for want of a minister. It is not revealed where he was. Perhaps indulging his morbid fancies in the ruinous manse which was soon to be demolished. Despite his mental resignation he lived on, in no better condition, until 1730. This is the dismal state to which much of Scotland was reduced by extreme Calvinistic doctrine. On March 3, 1701, the Records of the Session (in the Scottish Records Office, Edinburgh) sum up that critical situation as follows :—

The session having taken to their consideration the present sad state of the paroch through the Extraordinary indisposition of the Minister since the 18th of Januarie 1700 years and that by all human probation now have no ground to expect if ever he may be capable to exercise a ghospell ministrie amongst us ; Therefore have judged it our dutie to make application to the presbytrie to putt us in a condition for settling a ghospell minister amongst us, and to that effect wee appoint Mr. Robert Woomyss of Grange moore Hendrie Lamont Wm Allan and Wm., Lundin to attend the first presbitry after the arise of the present General Assembly."

They were not in any desperate hurry to act, however, and in the long interim before December 30th 1702, various preachers, some probationers among them, were induced to conduct services at long intervals. On the above date, Mr. Andrew Burn, an M.A. of St. Andrews, aged 26, is in the records as " preacher of the ghospell entered upon his tryalls." He successfully stood up to his ordeal and on Apryle 1st 1703 he was ordained.

The sermon which accompanied his ordination was preached by James Knox, minister of " Dunnino," whose very pointed text was from Acts, Chapter 20, verse 28, " Take heed therfore unto yourselves and to all the flock over which the Holy Ghost hath made you overseers to feed the church of God which he hath purchased with his blood."

On the following day the new minister and his session got down to brass tacks and " opened the box." which had been accumulating offerings for a long time.

It contained as follows :

Of silver money	£138	13s	08d
Of copper money	£13	06s	00d
Of bullion two ounces thirteen Troy sold for	£8	08s	00d

This was four years before the recall of the £900,000 which was all the currency, of assorted kinds, including counterfeit and foreign money, that existed in Scotland before the Union. The coinage had been progressively so debased by adulteration, not to speak of vast amounts of counterfeit metal, that, when it came to be linked up with sterling, the Scots pound was only value for one shilling and eight pence English money. Andrew Burn could not forsee this event, so, for him and his session, the box represented a windfall, even though it was made up of a hotch-potch of marks, bodles, turners, hardheads and bawbees. A year or two ago I picked up a small piece of copper money in the garden of the Old Manse and had it inspected at the National Museum of Antiquities. They pronounced it to be a turner, or twopenny piece of the reign of Charles I, minted under licence at Stirling in 1632 - 3 and not counterfeit. It was thin, the size of our present half-penny, and the impresssion worn but readable. Its value as sterling would be one-sixth of an English penny, but such coins were frequently given as alms to itinerant poor, or offered by poor parishioners for the collection ladle.

Chapter VII

MANSE OF 1703

TO accommodate the new minister and to compensate for three years' neglect, owing to Thomas Black's disorder, a new manse had to be built in a traditional style, narrow, long and high. Such a style had several advantages, as well as disadvantages, but it was economy rather than comfort that dictated the style of building. Stone was cheap and readily available in the ruins of the former manse and in the freestone strata nearby on the shore, much of which was limestone, which could be burnt for mortar with the seams of coal found amongst the limestone. Masons' labour was not dear, and there were many skilled masons at hand. Long timber was available, being much used in the ship-yards, but a narrow roof could use short timber and this was more likely to stand up to storms. The smaller roof required fewer tiles which, though manufactured in several places on the east Coast, were often imported from Flanders as a kind of ballast to be replaced by exports of grain, malt and salt-fish. The use of slate was not common (except in a few areas where it was locally quarried), until it could be transported by sea and later by rail from the Welsh or Highland slate quarries.

The first slates were those brought by sailing vessels from Ballachulish, or Easdale, on the Argyll coast. They were dark, hard, thick and durable. Easdale is an island entirely made of slate. It was intensively worked from about 1650, the highly esteemed slates being carried by sea to Glasgow and other sea-ports. There being no Caledonian Canal until the mid-nineteenth century, it was a laborious business to bring Argyll slates to Anstruther, but this was done. In 1789 the roof of Anstruther Easter Kirk was repaired with Argyll slates ; and in 1761 the Kirk and manse of Anstruther Wester were both repaired with Easdale slates. These are still on the Manse.

Obviously the warmest kind of house is circular or square. The long, high, narrow manse required a fire in every room, coal being cheap and plentiful, and servant-lassies to carry it upstairs were not in short supply either. The Manse has nine rooms, three to each storey ; the nine chimneys are in threes, at the gables and nearer the centre. To compensate for the chilly winds and sea-fogs, the walls are three feet thick, with rubble centres, quite common in any old Scottish houses that were not built to stand a cannonade. The interior staircase, spiralling clockwise, or diesel, was of wood, unlike the staircase of the 16th century manse of Anstruther Easter where the staircase was originally of stone, in a central pillar built up of the inner ends of the steps ; a remarkable piece of masonic artistry. Apart from slight alterations and additions made before the middle of this century, the manse of Anstruther Wester still stands, still inhabited, as it was when Andrew Burn took up residence in Apryle, 1703.

He was to live and minister here for 57 years, during the earlier part of which his wife bore him eleven children : Elizabeth, George, Partick, Janet, John, Andrew, Jean, Andrew, John, David, Janet. The first Janet, John and Andrew died in childhood, cause not recorded, but, from their being of about the same ages, probably of some infectious disease such as scarlet fever, diphtheria or dysentery : but they were resurrected in the flesh, if not in a theological sense, in a second trio bearing the same names but in reverse order. Even two centuries off, it is still poignant to read of this attempt at consolation.

During Burn's very long ministry, earth-shaking events were taking place of which only a few tremors reached the Old Manse. The Union of 1707, with its nationwide mob violence against the " parcel of rogues in a nation ", who were " bought and sold for English gold ", certainly had its repercussions in Fife. Before the English Revolution of 1688, as we saw earlier, the ministers were almost solidly " agin the government " and the lairds were known, collectively, as the " whig Lairds of Fife." Some of the lairds, indeed, carried this fanatical hatred of the Establishment to the length of murder most foul.

In the parish church, South Street, St. Andrews, is an enormous marble memorial, made in Holland, showing in grim detail, in bas-relief, the barbarous murder of Archbishop Sharpe on Magus Moor, three miles outside the town, in 1679; Sharpe had spent the previous night in the Manse of East Anstruther. The chief agent in this crime was Hackstoun of Rathillet, an East Neuk laird, backed up by Balfour of Burleigh, a descendant of one of the most illustrious ancient Fife lines. Their accomplices were drawn from other lairds and assorted fanatics, who all came to as violent an end as their revered victim. This memorial is most remarkable. It is in the heavy formal Carolean style, showing Dutch influence and workmanship. The epitaph is in Latin marmoreal in which the assassins are not spared. It was completed and erected in the autumn of 1679, a very rapid piece of work, for the Battle of Bothwell Brig, which put an end to the rising brought on by the murder of Sharpe, had been fought on Midsummer's Day of that year. It is a paradox that, in the vestibule of the parish kirk which houses this vehement condemnation of

Presbyterian violence, the porch is dedicated to John Knox, who initiated such use of force. My personal taste in the memorials here is not religious. It is the simple memorial to Tom Morris, senior, the great golfer, an elder here for many years. It sums him up superbly as the epitome of a good Fifer ; " Generous in rivalry, modest in victory."

When the Whigs came into power in 1688, the Fife lairds and some ministers turned Jacobites and were " out " in the '15 and '45 risings. They seem to have taken a perverse delight in backing the political underdogs. I mentioned, earlier, Thomas Auchinleck, for a brief time the minister of Anstruther Wester, who was a Jacobite, and as usually happened, an Episcopalian at heart. But Andrew Burn was of a different stamp. Whatever his private feelings, he did not go off on a wild goose chase, but kept far from war's alarm, perhaps having in his mind a text from Hudibras,

Alas, what perils do environ
The man who meddles with cold iron.

The rising, however, did affect East Fife. Rob Roy, after his neutral role at Sheriffmuir, led a party of his caterans and occupied Falkland Palace, where he and his men hibernated with all the crude luxuries of early Stuart kings, and lived at large on stolen cattle and other goods " reived " from the Howe of Fife. Their raids did not extend to Anstruther, but parties of Highlanders appeared in the East Neuk towns and prevented the regular church services from being held. These bands of Jacobites, prohibited from crossing the Forth at Stirling, were seeking sea-passage to Lothian. As they were notorious thieves, they made the Fife Whigs very anxious about their movables.

In 1736 there occurred an incident which, as I indicated earlier, showed the violent dislike of the Scots for the excise. Many a time they wished for what Robert Burns (himself forced to earn his bread as a Preventive Officer) put into song, that " The Deil would be awa' wi' the Exciseman." In Pittenweem, the Excise Collector, who was lodging immediately west of the Town House in St. Mary's Street, and therefore in direct contact with law and order, was robbed by Wilson and Robertson of £200, realised from the sale of confiscated goods. Perhaps the magistrates of Pittenweem had a repute for timidity similar to those of Anstruther Wester of whom it was said, " instead of being a terror to evil-doers, evil-doers were a terror to them." As is well-known from Scott's " Heart of Midlothian ", this Pittenweem robbery with violence led to the famous Porteous Riots in Edinburgh, wherein all classes of the city took over the judiciary and the executive from the government in London, and executed Porteous in a " kangaroo trial," but in a disciplined if summary manner. The national sympathies were with the East Neuk law-breakers.

Chapter VIII

HIGH JINKS IN ANSTER

WHILST on the subject of lawlessness it would be appropriate to mention some things, which, if not exactly infringements of the penal code, were regarded as showing how much original sin continued to manifest itself, especially in Anstruther, despite the general " Hypocrisy " which, according to Thomas Carlyle (who taught in Kirkcaldy for as long as his brittle patience held out) was rampant, along with " Atheism and the Ghoul Sensuality " in the 18th century.

The Fife folk had always responded to merry-making, music, dancing and practical joking. One of the funniest poems to be found in Scots literature, which abounds in rumbustious humour, is one I have already quoted, " The Wife of Auchtermuchty," which was old in 1768, when it was universally known, and thought to have been composed by an unknown genius in the reign of Mary Queen of Scots, or earlier. The language is now too antique for our anglified generations. It was simplified and ruined by Allan Cunningham in a mealy-mouthed version entitled " John Crumlie ", which entirely misses the robust language and humour of old Fife, that the presbyterian church did its best to bowdlerise or suppress. There was no such suffocation in mediaeval times : the older churchmen had their faults, but they saw to it that the natural human instinct to have a roaring good time now and again, preferably now, was associated with holy days and holy fairs. The Great St. Andrews Fair, or Senzie Fair, lasted for fifteen days. The name Senzie is the old French Seinie, meaning a synod ; the fair being held in the great square of the cathedral. Two of the relics of St. Andrews three fairs each year are still celebrated ; one, indirectly, in the Kate Kennedy procession on the date of the old April fair, and the other, the Senzie, in August, when according to the local saying, " A' thing dees after the Lammas Fair," which may have a psychological as well as a natural meaning.

But, in olden times, both in St. Andrews and in Anstruther, a' things were not allowed to dee. Both of these towns had three fairs per annum. Anstruther's were in April, July and November. These were uproarious occasions, so racily described in " Anster Fair," by the poet William Tennant, in 1812. The famous Drummond of Hawthornden found time, from writing his classical masterpieces and lamenting the tragic loss of his lady-love, to go round Fife, especially the East Neuk, in the early 17th century, and note the " carrying-on " of the merrymakers there. His poem (though it has never been proved that he was the author) is a ludicrous mixture of Latin and Scots, entitled " Polemo - middinia,"or a " Treatise on Middens." Anstruther is faintly disguised as Anstraea, famed for such fish as " haddocus ", " codlineus," " lobster mony-footus." Some of the local worthies may still be recognised in re-incarnations as " Rob Gib, wantonus homo," " plouky-faced Watty Strang," " Willie Dick heavi-arstus homo," all of whom were in the habit of tripping it lightly in jolly dances and jigs, and also keen on " bonnaeas lassas kissare."

The famous song, " Maggie Lauder," is one of the liveliest Scottish songs. It is attributed to Francis Sempill, a 17th century poet.

> " Meg up and walloped ower the green
> For brawly could she frisk it."

She lived in the East Green of Anstruther some time before 1650 ; this we know, because, in the above song, reference is made to the famous piper Habbie Simson, who died and was lamented in notable stanzas by Robert Sempill, Francis' poetical father, about that period. Some mealy-mouthed writers say that " Maggie practised not the most reputable of professions " which could mean almost any profession, but is meant to suggest that she was a whore, and kept a " house of ill-repute " in East Green. Others say she was related to the local aristocracy. These allegations are not necessarily contradictory, though it is gilding her character rather much to call her the " Lily of the Bass," unless this means that she had the morals of a solan goose. The site of her cottage is now a rock-garden, with benches ; what was once facetiously described as a " sitooterie."

When James V visited Anstruther about 1540 the Dreel was in spate and he, in the words of the ballad, " was laith to weet his cork-heeled shune," so he got a pick-a-back from a sturdy beggar-lass, with whom he struck up in amorous acquaintance, a common habit with the early Stuart kings. On the basis of this incident a convivial club was set up in Anstruther, with off-shoots in neighbouring Fife towns and in Edinburgh. It was named " The most Ancient and Puisant Order of the Beggar's Bennison and Merryland." (original spelling). Its minute books were printed in Anstruther in 1892 for private circulation. A copy may be inspected on request to the Keeper of Manuscripts in the National Library of Scotland, if good and sufficent reason is adduced. Perhaps this demi-secrecy is as well for the reputations of the subscribers to those Hell-fire clubs, who passed in daylight for respectable lairds, merchants and ministers. Ladies of pleasure were recruited for these secret saturnalias from all the " confines of the Horestii." Nobody in the know could with cause accuse Anstruther of being a dull, straitlaced community. In fact, it was reputed to be the most drunken town on the coast. The two parishes, East and West, in Andrew Burn's time, had upwards of eighty brewsters, mostly women. There is a story told of one of these ladies, that, on being caught canoodling with an exciseman, by her husband, she calmly informed him, " Weel, sic things maun happen when ye sell ale." There was every encouragement for determined sociality, but, of course, never on a Sunday, unless far up a wynd where the perambulating elders were unlikely to penetrate.

In view of the above we can credit that Andrew Burn had much to occupy himself with, quite apart from any political events.

According to the session records, he and his elders had their hands full, dealing with the domestic upsets of Anstruther Wester. The Kirk of that period was obsessed with sex, that is to say, with searching out, reprimanding, and suppression of irregularities in that basic human need. Over and over again, week after week, with boring repetition, they had to deal with pre-nuptual fornication, casual fornication, adultery, disputed paternity. Apparently men were drawn to Anstruther for carnal gratification from such far-away and joyless regions as Dunino, Abercrombie, Kilconquhar, and even Elie, Earlsferry and St. Andrews ; in which case the ministers of these parishes had to co-operate, and set the guilty upon the cutty-stool of repentance, dressed in penitential linen.

One Anstruther lady said in the inquisition that she could not identify her lover, the said fornicator having addressed her in the obscurity of an October night. Pressed further, she insisted she could not be sure who he was, at which impasse two elders were deputed to interview all suspects, a task which would have taxed both Solomon and Agag.

The women of the parish, and, less frequently, the men, were haled up for swearing, scolding, brawling and bandying about such names as " whore," to the general disturbance, leading to " canallies," or tumults. Offenders, for these and other peccadillos, were often imprisoned in the church steeples, to encourage more elevated behaviour.

Chapter IX

WITCHCRAFT

WITCHCRAFT was still being practised, or at least suspected of being practised, by both sexes. One male suspect, brought before the session, was charged with raising spells by digging a deep hole by lamplight on a piece of waste ground. Nearly all Scottish villages allowed a piece of waste ground to remain uncultivated. This was named the " Gudeman's Croft " or the " Deil's Gairden " and was dedicated to the forces of evil. It was probably in such a plot that the suspect was digging. His lame excuse was that he was searching for a piece of " lymme-stane " to build into a wall. A likely story.

Pittenweem had a bad reputation for witch-hunting and, when this was frowned on by the law, executing mob-justice on poor deranged creatures. In Burn's early ministry, only a short distance beyond the parish, a wretched old woman was crushed to death by being trampled by a mob. It is recorded in a ballad of the time, "The Witch of Pittenweem," that the witch-hunters spared themselves no trouble to prosecute their sport. They carried their victims for three Scots miles to the place of execution.

" They took her to Kinniuchar Loch
And threw the limmer in
And a' the swans took to the hills
Scar'd wi th'unhaely din."

There are innumerable ballads composed on such events, soon after their happening. Of such are " The Witch of Eildon " and " The Witches and Warlocks o' Edincraw " where no obscene details are spared.

There is a Witches' Wynd only a stone's throw west of the Old Manse of Anstruther Wester, its name not bestowed by pure fantasy. The last witch burned by a Scots kirk session was in Dornoch in 1722, but this was very late in history for an official " incremation ". There were, however, instances of mob witch-burning, for example, in Hertfordshire, not twenty miles from London, as late as 1751, the guilty instigators being hanged. But, only two years after Andrew Burn's induction, there was a mass burning of witches by the kirk session of Spott, near Dunbar, just across the Firth. When the Act prohibiting this barbarism was passed by Parliament in Westminster, the Associate Synod of the Church of Scotland, composed of the residue of the non-juring Cameronians, regretted this latitudinarian step, quoting the Old Testament to support them, from the text "Thou shalt not permit a witch to live." Dr John Brown of Haddington, in an article in his well-known Bible Dictionary, used far into the 19th century, still persisted in demanding the death penalty for witches.

The sad chapter of history on witchcraft has always fascinated people on account of its paradox. When modern European history began, about 1500, and men's minds were enlightened by the rediscovery of classical learning, witches were officially condemned for the first time by the Catholic Church. In 1484 a papal bull gave official sanction to witch-hunts. A hundred years later, in presbyterian Scotland, the hunts were in full cry, and continued unabated for a century or more. Lothian was notorious for incremations, Fife equally so. The belief died hard. As late as the early 19th century a man averred that he has been seized upon near the Calliard, or Old Hag's Hill between St Monan's and Elie. The carlines had carried him seven times round Kinniuchar Loch, a total of ten miles air-borne in all, before depositing him on terra firma ; a sobering experience.

To show how superstitious ordinary folk were, quite late in history, we have the evidence of the clergyman of Ceres, near Cupar. Lunardi, the famous balloonist, made a flight from Heriot's Hospital in Edinburgh in 1785, was carried north, and passed slowly over Fife, landing near Ceres. The minister wrote to an Edinburgh newpaper; " The sight gave much pleasure to such as knew what it was, but terribly alarmed such as were unacquainted with this celestial vehicle."

John Knox, even at his most demoniacal peak, was not accused of being a warlock, yet, according to a report, he was banished from St. Andrews in 1570, two years before his death, for emulating the witch of Endor, and raising spirits out of the earth in his backyard, whereby, on the Evil One himself coming up, Richard Bannatyne, a servantman, died of fright. This may be a libel on the great reformer, for he had many ecclesiastical enemies; there is a parallel tale, recounted as a true one, by Scott of Scotstarvit, near Ceres. He writes that in Edinburgh, in 1541, a warlock, Richard Graham, raised the devil, literally, in his backyard in the Canongate and a spectator died at the success of his necromancy.

All the Fife burghs have records of the supernatural. In addition, many natural objects were regarded with awe and terror. Hares, swine, salmon, skate, bum-clocks, (flying-beetles) and deil's coachmen (cockroaches) were objects of horror. But, if Miss Muffet had lived in St. Monan's, she would have eaten her curds and whey quite unmoved, for spiders were tolerated there, as indeed all over Scotland, for they were supposed to have rapidly spun their webs over caves where saints were hiding, or to have inspired Bruce to greater feats of perseverance.

Apart from these debts of gratitude, many of the phobias seem to be derived from Jewish taboos in Leviticus, where hares, swine, scale-less fish, etc. were unclean. Or the prohibitions may be of even stranger origins, going back to ancestral customs. Harry (later Heinrich) Heine, the German Jewish poet asked, " What are the Scots but a pork-eating tribe of Jews ? " But few Scots ate pork. A British tribe called the Gadeni, (soft g) whose chief fortress was Jedworth, now Jedburgh, are said to have given their name to Inchkeith, an island belonging to the parish of Kinghorn. The ancient name was Caer Guidi, according to the Venerable Bede, who lived in the 7th century. This means the fort of Judes, which must have existed in the earliest centuries of the era. It was built of wood, and as the soil of Inchkeith is fertile, and springs numerous, this fort must have been impregnable. These tribesmen may possibly have been derived from bands of Jewish slaves, exiled by Hadrianus. It is an archaelogical truth, recently discovered, that, while the towns of the Ottadini, a neighbouring tribe, were spared by Hadrianus, he completely devastated the hill-towns of the Gadeni. Excavations recently on Torwoodlee, the Gadeni fort above Galashiels, reveal that it was burnt by the Romans, along with its inhabitants. In view of Hadrian's known hatred of the Jews there is a strong suspicion that he had an unreasonable spite against the Gadeni. The early history of Scotland holds many mysteries and tales of incredible bravery and atrocity. Bannockburn is well-publicised, but who knows or cares about the equally terrific conflicts waged in Fife. For example, at Loch Ore, in the shadow of Ben Arty, where the Horestii assaulted Agricola's camps and were only repulsed after a bloody battle.

To strike a lighter and more humorous note, which may or may not prove the ancestry of the St. Monan's folk, the minister was preaching early last century on the subject of the Gadarene swine invested by evil spirits. The text was given out: "Then went the devils out of the man and entered into the swine." As the preacher spoke the last word, the muttered exorcism, "Cauld airn!" rang through the pews and everyone reached for a nail or a knife. As the sermon proceeded, the abhorred word was again uttered, and produced an alarming growl of " Cauld airn ! " But it was more than flesh and blood could stand when the worthy man mentioned swine for the third time. The entire congregation rose and " skailed " in a panic into the open air. In John Brown's Dictionary he says that the Jews so abhorred swine that they could not bear to hear the very word spoken.

In Buckhaven, which as I said is reputed to have been founded in the 16th century by Flemish mariners, there were many ludicrous incidents, if we are to believe Dugald Graham's book on the "Sayings of Wise Willy and Witty Eppie," published in chapbook form in the mid-eighteenth century. The braying of a donkey caused a terrible panic. The villagers timorously approached the asinine trumpeter and finally decided that, as he had the long ears of a hare and was of such an unnatural size, he must be Beelzebub himself, the father of such evil beasts as flies, hares, (or bawds) and bum-clocks. Graham's book if full of such "bawdy" tales of nonsense.

One of the earliest witches to be burnt, long before the Reformation, was Witch Grizzie (or Grizelda) condemned in St. Monan's in about 1490. The barbarous custom was to "worry" the poor wretches at the stake to prevent them from dozing off. But Grizzie, incredibly, fell asleep, and vanished into thin air in the shape of a bum-clock, an insect still locally called a "Deil's Horse".

Although somewhat along the coast from the East Neuk, it shows the nature of religion in the High Middle Ages, when it is truthfully recorded of the parish priest of Inverkeithing in the thirteenth century, that, in order to celebrate the feast of St. Priapus, he ordered out all the maidens of the town to perform ritual dances, naked, beneath the probably disapproving glimpses of the moon.

As Burn's long ministry went on, a more sceptical, but tolerant atmosphere prevailed. The 1745 rising did not much affect Anstruther though some of the lairds were Jacobites. The ministers prayed mightily for the non-success of Bonnie Prince Charlie, and no doubt thought, in April 1746, when the news of the butchery at Culloden came through, that they had done a good job.

Chapter X

BRIGHT SPIRITS

Andrew Burn died, full of years, aged 84, in 1760. His successor was a bachelor, Andrew Waddell. He must have been something of a new broom. He considered that the octogenarian had let things slide, particularly the roof-tiles, for we read that both the Old Manse and the Kirk were repaired and re-roofed in 1761. But otherwise Waddell does not seem to have stirred up trouble for himself or others. He died unmarried in 1767, perhaps to the chagrin of a few nubile spinsters in the parish.

James Forrester, only 24, fresh from St. Andrews College, was inducted in 1768. He was to remain for thirty years and to come in contact with many illustrious and worthy people. The dynasty of the Nairnes held sway in the Anstruther Easter parish for the entire 18th century. There were three generations, James (1690-1771), John (1711-1795), and James (1750-1819); each in turn becoming Father of the Presbytery of St. Andrews, as Forrester was to be in his turn.

John Nairne's daughter, Jean, born three days before Robert Burns, on 22nd January 1759, was married to James Forrester after he had been ten years in the Old Manse. No doubt, in view of the longevity of her family, she was expected to survive to be the matriarch of the manse. But nine months after her marriage

> "Came the blind Fury with th'abhorred shears
> And slit the thin-spun life."

She was sweet-and-twenty. It is hard to imagine with what effort Forrester managed to inhabit the manse and share it at all seasons, in the long June twilights, and when the winter storms sent the German Ocean roaring through the night over the near-by skellies, with that gentle ghost, companion of his brief spell in Eden, "playful no longer, as had been her habit."

After some years he married again and his wife bore him three children.

Both before and after his marriage in 1778, he and the Nairnes were much in and out of the twin parish manses. Present at some of these social gatherings was one of the strangest men that Scotland has ever produced, and that is a pretty rash statement. He was William Wilkie, professor of Natural Philosophy in the University of St. Andrews, a subject which then comprehended most of the sciences, as well as engineering practice and the embryo studies of electricity and magnetism. Wilkie's private enthusiasm in practical work was the growing of potatoes and turnips in his farm at Cameron, from which hobby he gained the nickname "Potato Wilkie." Potatoes were for long treated as delicate exotic plants, rather as tomatoes now, but in 1746 they were grown successfully in the open field in Midlothian. In the 1760's William Wilkie was growing them in bulk.

He had been appointed to St. Andrews in 1759, perhaps the appointment having been influenced by the fame of his nine-book epic on the descendants of seven Greek heroes of Homeric times. This chef-d'oeuvres was named the "Epigoniad" and was immediately, and for a generation after, praised to the skies by David Hume and other Scots, as a supreme work of genius. The author was named "The Scottish Homer". On a less elevated theme he wrote "Moral Fables in Verse", only one, "The Partan and the Hare", being in his native tongue, the metropolitan Scots of Lothian, not unlike Fifish. His father had been minister of Ratho, and he must often have been at a loss to deal with his eccentric offspring, of whom an eminent contemporary said, "His character, more than anyone he had known, was near the two extremes of a god and a brute." The story is told that Wilkie, when a student, was sent out with his Greek and Hebrew books and a musket to scare the wood-pigeons off his father's corn, which his ragged garments would have done, without fire-arms. An Edinburgh savant, passing to the ferry with a learned English scholar, knowing of Wilkie's reputation for erudition, told his guest that in Scotland learning was universal, and every peasant was fluent in Greek, Latin and Hebrew. His friend was frankly incredulous and said so, whereat the savant stopped the coach and took his guest across to the scarecrow. In no time Wilkie was deep in classical quotations, and soon the sceptic was out of his depth and eventually extricated himself from the discussion. He did not at all appreciate being humbled by a Scottish tatty-bogle.

This was the man who visited the Anstruther manses frequently from 1759 to 1772, when he died prematurely, despite his great attention to his health, which he guarded assiduously by sleeping with twenty-four pairs of blankets over him, winter and summer. From 1768, for over three years, Wilkie was accompanied on these walks across the hill from St. Andrews, a mere six Scotch miles (9½ English) by his favourite student, the brilliant, humour-loving poet Robert Fergusson. Some of the more sober professors did not much love Fergusson's mercurial temperament, and he was once or twice disciplined. Many of his pranks merit recalling. The aptest is his grace, at which as a divinity student he had to take his turn, over the monotonous diet of rabbits, which the College had the privilege of trapping on the West Links. Before he could be interrupted, Fergusson intoned in a sanctimonious voice:

For rabbits hot and rabbits cold,
For rabbits young and rabbits old,
For rabbits tender and rabbits tough,
Our thanks we render, we've had enough.

Amen.

On the way across to Anstruther, passing over the King's Muir of Dunino, the pair of wags heard that a young man was lying sick of tertian fever in a near-by cottage. Fergusson pretended to be a doctor of medicine, visited the sick man, took his pulse, inspected his tongue and prescribed some quite innocuous draught of herbs from the garden, but would take no fee, to the cottager's surprise.

One can imagine how well such tales were received round the fireside at either of the manses, with screeds of satirical and lyrical verse from these lively spirits. One of the favourite rooms for these seances was the "Watch Tower" of the Anstruther Easter Manse, a small room high up, looking splendidly south over the silver Forth on to the green champaigns of Lothian. It was on this view that Fergusson based his matchless thumbnail sketch of Edinburgh, nearly thirty miles away, but clearly seen against the Pentland Hills.

Aft frae the Fifan Coast I've seen
Thee tow'ring on thy summit green;
So glow'r the saints when first is given,
A fav'rite keek o' glore and heaven;

Fergusson was undergoing a course at St. Andrews, a curriculum he was never destined to finish, owing to the sudden death of his father, which compelled him to return to the drudgery of clerking, and, eventually, through a brain-fever following a fall, to a nightmarish end, gambolling and blaspheming in the straw in the Darien House, so far reduced as to be Edinburgh's Bedlam.

What would we not give to have a record of these meetings in the parlours of the Old Manses? Or to have any mementos of these geniuses, so soon to be obliterated for long by the sheer shameful weight of national neglect? Only by the chance of Burns commemorating his debt to

Fergusson was that brilliant boy's reputation restored. No one has so far done anything for poor Wilkie, who wrote prophetically:

> "Ossian's deathless strains . . .
> With modern epics share one common lot
> This day applauded and the next forgot."

Of such illustrious events was the early ministry of Forrester compounded. There was, however, during this period, a very great contrast between these visitors at the manse and the ordinary folk of Anstruther Wester. The town, created a royal burgh by James IV in 1587, four years after a similar honour had been granted to Anstruther Easter, has been in decline for over a century, and seemed on the verge of extinction. Forrester was often hard put to it to furnish the poor with charity out of the meagre income of the church. At that time Christian charity was dispensed in all cases of need, irrespective of any moral judgement on the applicant. There was no category, as there was in Victorian times, of the undeserving poor. Even beggar vagrants, who happened to die in passing through a parish in Scotland, were buried in a Christian manner at church expense. It makes sad reading to go over the straits that the session of Anstruther Wester were driven to, by the ruin of East Fife, due largely to political jealously of the English and Dutch merchants and government. Disasters at sea also were part of the accepted scheme of things; to provide for these there were two boxes, the Fisherman's and the Captain's, controlled by independent bodies, and replenished by various ways such as rentals of land, including, for the Captain's Box, the rental of Cameron Farm, tenanted for a time by Wilkie. But the ordinary poor were often saved from sheer starvation by small contributions from the session.

Across the Dreel Burn in 1771 occurred an event, the consequences of which were to split Scotland from stem to stern seventy years later. John Chalmers and Elizabeth Hall were married on 20th August. Their son Thomas was the bold minister who defied the Establishment, and led the dissidents out of St. Andrew's Church, Edinburgh, in 1843, to form the nucleus of the Free Church. Forrester could hardly have foreseen what tremendous events were being prepared only a stone's throw away from the Old Manse. Today, Chalmer's birthplace, neglected and weed-grown, makes a very just commentary on Scotland's interest in many of her great souls who braved the dust and heat to run for the immortal garland.

Chapter XI

STORMY PETREL

Forrester's final years in Anstruther Wester, as the century closed in war, revolution and political unrest, kept a fairly even tenor. But a very stormy petrel from the Hebridean seas was meantime winging his way towards the Old Manse. Through the patronage of the laird, Anstruther himself, and the influence of several powerful friends, including the notorious Lord Braxfield, (the original of R. L. Stevenson's "Weir of Hermiston"), this brilliant young Aberdeen graduate, James Macdonald, whose native place was Paible in Uist, was ordained in Anstruther Wester in 1799. Let us not think that Forrester was thrown out after thirty years. Far from it; he was, in a sense, kicked upstairs to Kilrenny, "to ride a mile away," on a stipend double that of Anstruther Wester's £200 per annum. He enjoyed his new charge for ten years, dying in 1808.

James Macdonald, the new incumbent, was a handsome bachelor of 27. He had known no language but Gaelic until he was twelve. At Aberdeen, where most Highland students studied, not necessarily intending to graduate, Macdonald had mastered English, Latin, Greek and Hebrew; he was a brilliant linguist, not to be wondered at, for Gaelic is one of the languages allied to Latin, French, Spanish and Italian. It was said of him that, when he was minister of Anstruther, he knew as many languages as there were states in the United States of America, thirteen at that time. In his ministry, nevertheless, twelve of these would be unused, and his Highland pronunciation of English would probably be regarded by his congregation as a foreign tongue. Like St. Columba when he came among the Picts in the 6th century, and needed St. Comgall and St. Cainnech to be his interpreters, Macdonald, facile as he was, could not easily have understood broad Fife. In fact, he was like a fish out of water in Anstruther. As he sat reading in his garden he would hear the screaming of the gulls, reminding him of his home in Uist; on the other hand the wood-pigeons in the kirk-yard sycamores would remind him of the Gaelic interpretation of their soft cooing, "Cha'n ann de mo chuideachd thu," You are not one of my flock.

There are many Gaelic sayings about Macdonalds, true and untrue; but the one that comes nearest to a compliment is "Domhullach gun seoltachd," A Macdonald without cunning, a phenomenon never heard of. James Macdonald was intellectually very gifted, so he had all the mental equipment to be cunning if he chose: his actions, in certain crises of his short life, seem to show that he was most skilful in getting out of personal and political entanglements; but the quixotic chivalry he also was capable of, which ultimately destroyed him, shows he was not cunning in a bad sense. He was a strange mixture however, and while he was loyal to his chief, his wife, his bosom friends, he was not so to the political reformers, Muir, Skirving and Margarot, to whom he at first professed allegiance, and later accused of being actuated by the worst of motives. These affairs, however, were well away from the little world of Anstruther, which concerned him for over four years only.

A very erudite and well-researched book on James Macdonald was published about ten years ago by Professor Gillies of Leeds, who was able to obtain valuable information on the Anstruther period of Macdonald's life from the late Dr George Ogg. The book is entitled "A Hebridean in Goethe's Weimar," published by Blackwell. Anyone who wishes to follow the career of this most outstanding occupant of the Old Manse, should read it. I shall give only a few details as they concern our narrative.

Before being placed in Anstruther Macdonald had gained high repute in Germany, where his charm and intellect had won him friends among all the brilliant men and women who haunted the literary centre of Weimar. The dominent figure was the great Goethe, but there was a host of other scarcely lesser lights. At that time the poet Ossian, a heathen Gaelic poet of antiquity, had roused Europe into a Celtic renaissance. Even Napoleon, later, came under this spell. Here was a young man from the land of Ossian, who spoke Ossian's tongue, and recited Ossian's poems in the original, as well as the poems of the newly-dead Robert Burns. Macdonald was lionised, especially by the lionesses of Judah, who were undomesticated, and free to study in any direction they chose, unlike their Gentile sisters of Germany, for whom life was restricted to the three K's (in English, Cooking, Church and Children). These intellectual German Jewish ladies, like their French counterparts, had attained a full Women's Liberation before 1800, and were bound by no conventions. Their flattery and attentions would have turned many a man's head, let alone Macdonald's. He was gratified to the top of his bent. He now became the object of desire to a fascinating divorcee, a poetess, Emilie von Berlepsch, fifteen years his senior.

Only by the sheerest chance did I discover who Herr von Berlepsh was, for like Madame de Stael, another brilliant and notorious bluestocking of the time, the grey mare was the better horse ; their husbands were as obscure, biologically, as the male of a certain shrimp which spends its life in the left kidney of its dominant partner. Von Berlepsch, a Prussian junker or landowner, is known to fame, in apiarist circles only, as the inventor of a new kind of beehive. He must have proved a drone. His queen was now in full flight to capture Macdonald. But our Hebridean was well read in the scriptures, and decided that, though there appeared to be safety in numbers, there was much more in exodus. He returned to Scotland.

Although he says in his letters that he was contented in Anstruther Wester, having his books, a competency of £200 a year (paid partly in money) and no very heavy duties, he was never in any doubt as to his main objective in Fife. He had no intention of settling down to a long lifetime of ministering, as Andrew Burn had done. He had his eye on an academic appointment to one of the professorial chairs in St. Andrews, itself the metropolis of the area, which was described by Robert Chambers, in his walking-tour of Scotland in 1827, as " the carcass of its former glorious self." The number of students at the University rarely exceeded 140. Macdonald was obviously looking for a sinecure, wherein he could devote himself to literary labour, based on research, rather than on teaching. Although the blame for some of Fife's loss of prosperity could be laid squarely on the Creator's shoulders, the Auld Enemy, England, came in for a fair share of it. But, unluckily for Macdonald, the Highlanders, and particularly the Hebrideans, had been at the back of two of the worst Fife reverses. The first was the fate of the "Gentlemen Adventurers of Fife," to whom I referred earlier. They had been financed and equipped from Fife, had had the Royal blessing, and had tried to colonise Lewis and exploit its resources. Like the late Lord Leverhulme, their benevolence was unappreciated, perhaps with some cause. The noble soap baron was lucky ; he lost prestige and capital only : but the Gentlemen Adventurers lost their lives, were decapitated, and their salted heads sent back to King James in barrels, an insult he paid back in full. The second injury to Fife from the Highland quarter was again what I mentioned earlier. It was the total loss of all the Anstruther soldiers sent to face Montrose's Gaelic troops in 1645. In 1793 James Forrester noted, in the statistical account of the parish, that old people still spoke of relatives who had gone off to the wars and never returned.

The sins of the fathers are visited on the children, even unto the third and fourth generation : in 1799, when Macdonald arrived, the Lewis atrocity was six generations back, Kilsyth five ; but both were clearly remembered, as Forrester stated. If ever a man was requiring to outdo Agag in delicacy of walking, he was Macdonald in Anstruther.

But he chose to do far otherwise. Perhaps the fame he had acquired in Weimar, and to some extent in Edinburgh, then enjoying a Golden Age comparable to Weimar's, may have gone to Macdonald's head. After all he was an intimate, not only of the German intelligentsia, but of Scott, Jeffrey, Campbell and a host of brilliant literary, legal and medical figures. But this cut very little ice in Fife. The new minister frequently absented himself from his charge and from the meetings of the presbytery of St. Andrews of which he had, astonishingly, been made moderator, over the heads of several older and more experienced local men. To these sins of omission he added a monstrous indiscretion, to put it no worse.

Amongst reams of correspondence with continental friends he had continued, by pen, his friendship with Emilie von Berlepsch. She had pleaded with him to be allowed to visit Scotland. With a little discretion this could well have been arranged so that she could have resided with Macdonald's sister in Edinburgh (as she later did). By sailing packet, (for it was a few years before the service of steamboats in the Forth) Edinburgh was not far away, via Leith Pier. Some talk might have been occasioned, for Edinburgh was a sounding box then. But what matter ?" It's a far cry to Lochow." or in this case, to the Dreel. The notorious Madame de Stael had fallen madly in love with the very eminent Dr. Robert Robertson, an ornament of the cloth, and we can guess that, with such a lady, the affair would not have stopped at a few coy smiles over a fan. Edinburgh might have accommodated similar ministerial indiscretions.

But our bold Highlandman invited Emilie to stay with him in the Old Manse. In Germany she had openly flouted public opinion in her infatuation for Macdonald : in Anstruther the buzz went East and West the Toun in less time than it took to pronounce her name. What strange aliases Emilie acquired among the Fife folk, with the provocative name of Berlepsch, must be left to guess.

Macdonald avowed in correspondence that his motives were no other than those " actuated by humanity and chivalry," but if his association had been misconstrued in Weimar and Berlin, it was put down in the East Neuk generally as scandalously near fornication.

Emilie was well aware of the sensation she was causing. She records in her letters to intimates in Germany that she was certain that the inhabitants regarded her with the eyes of John Knox. Luckily for her they had better manners than that castigator of sin. Professor Gillies speculates, in his chapter on Macdonald's stay in Anstruther, on what would have been the effect on the parishioners had Macdonald arranged the visit of Madame de Stael to the manse, which he was all set to do, but which, in the end, he thought inadvisable on political grounds only, for about this time war with Imperial France had been renewed.

Eventually Emilie left in the huff to continue her travels in Scotland and to take notes for a travel book she contemplated publishing. In subsequent letters to Macdonald, some of which are preserved, she wrote very drily of his treatment of her. So his " humanity and chivalry " were ill-paid.

In 1803 Macdonald went to London, hoping for one of two church vacancies in the fashionable quarters of the city. But he failed to secure either. He attributed his rejection to two main prejudices against him : his political association with the German Liberals, and his personal friendship with Emilie. He was probably right. These were panic years in Britain ; the war was renewed, invasion was threatened, Ireland was in rebellion again, and there were many signs of social discontent, not unjustified.

In 1804 Macdonald announced, rather hypocritically, to the presbytery, that " Divine Providence had called him to discharge an important duty at a considerable distance from Anstruther." That was the end of his stay. He had never acclimatised himself to Fife. He did not like the ministers and said, perhaps with some truth, that they were all under the thumbs of their wives. Macdonald's father was a fine old man, well-known in the Hebrides as White Hugh, a name denoting his great head of snow-white hair. He lived to be about a hundred and many a time he must have shaken that head in sorrow over the chivalrous but tragic end of his son.

Although not now associated with the manse, here, briefly, is what happened to Macdonald. He travelled for a year or two as guide and tutor to two young Highland scapegraces, much in need of guidance ; young Clanranald, his own chief, and Ewan Murray MacGregor, heir to the disputed MacGregor chieftainship. After leaving Macdonald's protection Clanranald got himself into a scandal in Gothenburg in Sweden. An eccentric rich merchant there had a young wife inaptly named Constance ; who indiscriminately inflamed the depravity of " kings and brewers, princes and jews, counts and shopkeepers, Scots and Russians, Americans and Italians." Quite an international bag, into which Clanranald was also trawled. Despite the cold fact that he was £30,000 in debt, he offered £20,000 to the merchant for Constance. The scandal broke, and drew in the British premier Canning and George III. Macdonald volunteered to go and rescue his chief from the seductress, despite the fact that he had every good reason for remaining in Scotland, for he had recently married the spirited and amiable Janet Playfair, daughter of the Principal of St. Andrews University, and his academic ambitions appeared to be nearing achievement.

In November 1808, in a severe early winter, he set off from Leith to Gothenburg. The brig was wrecked on the desolate coast of Jutland. Macdonald with superhuman courage and effort saved the crew, and even went back for the captain's dog Chance. But Chance and Circumstance were not propitiated. After barbarous treatment from the hostile Danes, Macdonald reached Sweden to discover that the disreputable Clanranald had repented of his folly. Macdonald never got over his exposure to the savage elements and Danish jailers. He returned to Scotland, wrote feverishly and brilliantly on many topics, then, after a year, he died in a decline, probably tubercular, leaving his young bride only £16, and 54 years of widowhood to spend it in. Luckily she had other resources.

Chapter XII

THE END OF AN OLD SONG

MACDONALD'S successor was Andrew Carstairs, who reverted to orthodoxy. He was ordained in 1805, and settled to a lifetime of parish ministry. The times grew steadily worse as the Napoleonic War dragged on. Even after Waterloo the economy of Britain, the workshop of the world, cause widespread industrial and agricultural distress, leading to the massacre of " Peterloo ", and the severe repressions in Glasgow. The revolutions of 1830 and 1848 in Europe were no more effectual than the parallel riots in Scotland, which occurred in Fife also, for the " Hungry Forties " were severe on the weaving communities in the east of Scotland. The East Neuk, remaining tied to farming and fishing, did not fare quite so badly in those Dickensian days of workhouses and debtors' prisons and infant labourers.

Prosperity slowly returned until, in the mid-century, it is recorded that the tonnage registered in Anstruther was the highest in all the Scottish fishing-ports, 5000 persons employed, directly or indirectly, in the fishing industry. It was in this era that shipbuilding tonnage and horsepower on the Clyde exceeded the total of all other yards in Britain. The Forth was busy with steam and sail ; there were regular steam passages from Leith to Pittenweem and Anstruther on Mondays, Wednesdays and Fridays, the time taken being between two and three hours, as quickly as today by bus, the railway having been obliterated.

In his 31 years in the Old Manse Carstairs was twice married, and from these unions sprang twelve olive branches. In the intervals of domestic and parochial activity, he found time to write " The Scottish Common Service," and had a sermon included in Gibbon's " Scottish Pulpit," gone into the limbo of many devotional works. Rather belatedly he found the Old Manse damp, and incommodious for his many children. After over thirty years he moved into the new manse on the post-road to Pittenweem and on top of the fifty-foot beachline, well away from the salt spray. Here, however, he survived only two years.

Hew Scott moved into the new substantial square-built manse, and engaged himself upon a formidable task, at least as daunting as Dr. Johnson's Dictionary, and entailing far more laborious physical exertion, as well as mental obduracy. There were over nine hundred parishes in Scotland. Hew Scott visited every one of them to obtain from the very source all the detailed information of each, including the particulars of each minister, his life, and family and achievements. He did most of the journeying in summer, using scraps of envelopes and notepaper to take notes, and travelling by train, ship, coach or on foot over the wild terrain of highland parishes and the turbulence of Hebridean seas. His " Fasti Ecclesiae Scoticanae ", or " Calendar of the Church of Scotland ", covered all records from the Reformation to the date of his visit. It runs to many volumes, and although it has necessarily been brought up to date, it has rarely required to be amended. On the last day of 1871 he completed the last page, saying " My work is done." He never set foot outside again, and died in the following midsummer.

During the period of Hew Scott's incumbency, two literary celebrities visited Anstruther. Robert Louis Stevenson (originally Robert Lewis, the name being respelt owing to his father's anxiety not to be associated with an Edinburgh Bailie named David Lewis) spent some weeks in Anstruther in connection with his father's work on the harbour and May lighthouse, the Stevensons being renowned lighthouse engineers. He retained many impressions of the area, which he later used in his literary work. Mrs. Oliphant, who was to attain prominence as a popular and prolific novelist and miscellaneous writer, producing 120 volumes, wrote her first novel " Katie Stewart " about 1851. It had, as its locus, the town of Anstruther in the press-gang days of the Napoleonic Wars, and contains scenes which show that she must have had intimate knowledge of the area.

James Butchart, remembered yet by many of the old parishioners, ministered for 36 years, dying in 1908.

He was succeeded by James Paterson, who maintained the ministry of Anstruther Wester until the parish was united with Anstruther Easter in 1961. He did not long survive this union, dying in 1962. He is buried in the old kirkyard of his beloved parish.

Shortly after this the manse of 1836 was sold, and more recently it became celebrated under the picturesque name of the " Craw's Nest Hotel ", a reference to a jesting remark made by Charles II, when that Merry Monarch was being entertained in the Dreel Castle in an upper room overlooking the shore, which, on account of its dizzy position and its very limited space, reminded him of a crow's nest.

The original Manse of 1703 in now occupied privately, is fairly secluded, still close to the surge and thunder of the ocean, and wetted in storms by salt spray. Very few people trouble themselves to stir up its memories of glory, tribulation, scandal and piety.

THE END